Chronically Human

Abbie Strong

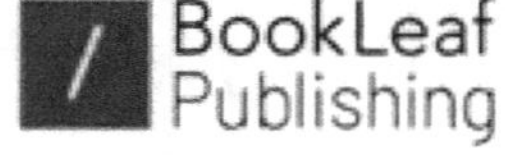

BookLeaf
Publishing

Presentation by *BookLeaf Publishing*

Web: www.bookleafpub.com

E-mail: info@bookleafpub.com

ISBN: 9789357210003

First edition 2022

Dear Me,

Dear Me,
        I want to start with our memory,
Remember what we did
What we became
Remember the shiver of January,
As frost bitten crystals blinded us from sight
Leading to the life of February,
Each ribbon and balloon, brought more joy than
imaginable
 Somehow you managed to dare March,
I dare you to do the unthinkable… don't think
just do it
And then, the rebirth of April
Just as the world began to bloom for spring so
did you
Imagine what came forth in May,
With a change in us came a Bing and a Bon
The too much to stop June,
Don't forget to tick, tick, tick… time keeps
moving you know
Surprise… it's July,
You did it, I dared you and you did it
Darkest of nights in heated August,
Silence is golden but… friendship is loud
On a ride to success in September,
Another year to begin and another one over

Boo… Got you October,
Be careful, of the ghosts, they're out
Not yet I know, November,
Don't rush the future you just need time
Another flight December,
You're finally back, don't forget it
Yours,
        Me
P.S. Remember You for Me.

Look Forward

You loved the idea eternally,
I loved you instead

The idea overtook you
And I suffered

I'm sorry for our time
I'm thankful for it too

Follow the idea and suffer
Look forward instead

Look forward
Please

The Girl in the Meadow

The girl in the meadow is nothing short of
stunning
Born in the beauty of nature itself
Floating as she danced
Feet barely gracing the tips of the grass
    Oh to be her again
Living for what is to be
The purest of white drapes her shoulders
Flowing past her ankles
Letting it float on the breeze behind her
A smile as bright as the sun itself
Auburn as the bark that surrounds me, her locks
tangled in an intricate knot
Deep as the unending ocean
Her emotions grasp me by a thread
Lost in the sound of time will we forever be
forgotten
I will forever remember the girl in the meadow
I used to be her, forgotten in the bow
Now happiness is not my own
It is hers…

A sacrifice as willing as a choice

See you again

I'd take a day to walk with you
See you again
Hear the music from your lips
Maybe add a few notes of my own
We'd talk for hours
I'd ask
      "How are you?"
      "Can you see me from up there?"

I see your shadow sometimes
Hear your laugh in a crowd
Feel your coats warmth in summer
Remember the games we would play

I'd take a day to talk with you
See you again
We'd swap tips in the garden
You'd wave at the gate

I'll see you again

The Girl in the Bow

The girl in the Bow began to weep
Forged from stone and earth
Grounded as a waterfall escaped from her soul,
fell
Trapped by the roots of her prison
She lives for me
Darkest of crimson flows down her body
She was our symbol of life
Her alabaster hair a nest from the past
Tangled to keep her place
I will forever remember the girl in the bow
One final whimper escapes her
A final whisper against the breeze

I reach a delicate hand out
Bloodstained fingers grab me

Let us dance now
The girl in the bow
Meets
The girl in the meadow
We shall dance for eternity

For we will be everlasting.

Rise

I watch as we fall
Yet like a phoenix you rise
Unlike you I crash

Endless

Crash into the stars
A constellation for all
Leading to the dark

Forsaken Envy

Winter's hold flows through me
A bittersweet claw
Brandishing a knife
A search to be free

Melodic crystals form throughout
Chimes to an invisible breeze
Wreaking havoc from within
Mountains creating a valley of doubt

Glaciers groan as the ice breaks
A steady stream of suspicion rising
A sickening vine of emerald overcomes
Watching as my heart aches

Forsaken as verdant vines cloud my vision
Frost making way to deathly fauna
Ice cold spiralling into heated envy
Creating an internal division

In a book...

There once was a child,
Who wanted more from life

She would reach for a world,
The weight was a relief.
A New Haven

Words a string of hope,
Tangling, tearing, teasing
A net of promises,
Catastrophically, captivating

Each sanctuary unique,
Euphoric, intoxicating
A Realm of Discovery,
Unknown, untouched, untried

A final ivory sheet turns,
Darkness, loss
Mourning;

A silver haired witch,
A queen in crimson,
A shapeshifting prince,
A king of a fallen kingdom,

'Only a promise to return again'

Clocks

How is a ghost of the past, the sight of the
future?
A travelling poltergeist of pain and misfortune,
Bringing luck and love and loyalty,
Leaving bad luck and loss and betrayal

What you did was nothing,
What I did was worse

And time ticks on
As the clock
Strikes
12

Divergent

Years have passed since I saw you last,
You don't know me
Nor I you

You were a child, and I a shell
A masked shell
Why did you save me

Although now I'm cursed,
To never know me,
Only to see from your eyes

I don't understand you
We have grown so far
    Apart

Blocked by my nature,
Trapped by my brain,
Lost to society?

How do I act?
Can I see what you feel?
I think I'm not typical

Emotions are a lie,

Body language, a falsehood
I think I'm divergent...

Dreams

There was once a girl who believed Wonderland
was home,
She tried every day to return
All she need do was close her eyes
And believe

There was once a boy who believed he could fly
Reach up,
        Step on the clouds,

He thought:
        A rocket,
            A balloon,
                A plane,
Little did he know, if only he jumped,
The clouds would come to him

Help Me

How is it I'm the one who "loses control"?
Even when you're the one pushing
Leaving whenever you want
Please don't leave me

My life is over without you
When I don't see you everyday

I am…

Today I'm a songbird,
Trapped in a wrought iron cage,

Agony unwillingly escaping,
Screaming to the world

My story an unstrung rope of pain,
Maybe one day I will be free
    Blue,
        Pain,
            Pink,
                Loss,
                    Purple,
                        Acceptance

Today I'm a canvas,
Displayed in a gallery of nothing

Joy, a kaleidoscope of colour,
Giggling with the world

My world of true colours shown,
Finally, I am free

Till then…

Like the rain,
You stayed for a short while,
Till I felt the sun

Then…

Like the sun,
You provided warmth,
Till I felt the burn

Then…

Like the burn,
You let me heal,
Till I felt the scar

Then like all scars
I will always remember

Ever notice?

Ever notice the girl at the back of the class?
Always silent, trapped within,
Screaming for no-one,
It was too late when you noticed her,
She moved on

Ever notice the boy at the bus stop?
Same stop, same time, every day,
Wishing for a bus that never comes,
When you did, he vanished
His bus came

Ever notice the couple in the coffee shop?
Cold coffee, warm tears,
Hoping for their child's return,
You felt that… they didn't get their
homecoming,
They were gone

Ever notice me?
Laughing, crying, shouting… being me,
A mask of who I am,
You did… eventually,

You

don't
notice
me.

Sold

Flames flicker,
Drifting breeze,
Lost control,
Light Frost,
Embers fall,
Ash flies,
Black mark,
Dark soul,

I didn't know these were signs of the devil,
Filling my heart till all was sold,
A soul darker than the night sky,
Filled with a cacophony of noise,
Sold to the frigid depths of nothing,
A Hollow beat

Ambition

Tell the world you will
Fly, finally you will soar
Let go of the cage

Brain Frog

I have a friend…
		Meet Brain Frog,
We get along…
		Sometimes

They enjoy telling me jokes…
		But only if you're talking,
They are quiet…
		Sometimes

I like to dance…
		They only spin to dance,
They are fun…
		Sometimes

Brain Frog and I argue…
		They don't like me to remember,
I get tired…
		Sometimes

That's my oldest friend…
		Thanks Brain frog,
We get along…
		Sometimes

The heart's currency

"Is my secret safe with you?"

Rain whispers a silent song as it falls,
A song of myths and legends,
A sweet sort of lullaby,
A rhythm from the heavens

A once heard symphony,
Rarely do they cry so loud,
Heart full of deceit and sorrow,
Yet, we hear their chorus

Angels guide the pain,
Hidden in an abyss of silence,
You keep some and give more,
A strange currency of the heart

"Only till the sky falls"

Endless

You cannot stare into its eyes,
What if you lose yourself?
Words beckon like a star within the dark
Then devour what you give